Robert D. Vandall

TAKE NOTE

11 Noteworthy Solos in a Variety of Styles for Elementary to Late Elementary Pianists

(UK Exam Grades 1–2)

Foreword

The goal of all teaching is to prepare students to learn on their own. There is nothing that I enjoy more than helping students discover how pieces are put together. Through such analysis, they can discover practice strategies and techniques that help them learn music quickly and accurately. Knowledge of the musical materials combined with effective practice techniques results in expressive and exciting performances.

Take Note, Book 1, contains 11 solos for elementary to late elementary pianists in a variety of styles, keys and tempi. Several of the solos have an optional teacher/parent duet that adds interest and excitement to the lesson and practice time at home. A special **Take Note** section is included for each piece. The comments and questions in **Take Note** help students find theoretical concepts and musical patterns in the piece. Rather than an extensive list of practice points, special features are noted. Then, students are asked to discover similarities and differences in the music that will lead to effective study and practice.

Enjoy!

Alfred Music
P.O. Box 10003
Van Nuys, CA 91410-0003
alfred.com

ISBN-10: 1-4706-2025-1
ISBN-13: 978-1-4706-2025-7

This piece is in A natural minor.

1. Both hands stay in one position for the entire piece
    except for m. 16 (the second time). Which hand moves? _____

    What note does it play? _____

2. The rhythm in m. 1 is used several times
    in the piece. In which measures is it used? _____

3. There are two harmonic intervals in
    the right hand. Name the intervals. _____

Push It!

Robert D. Vandall

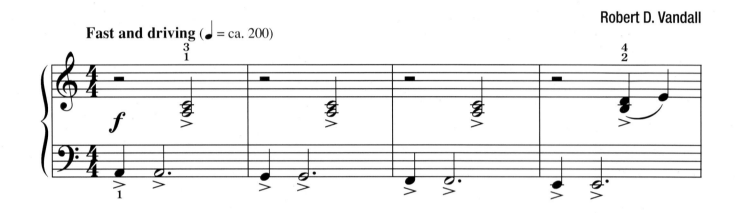

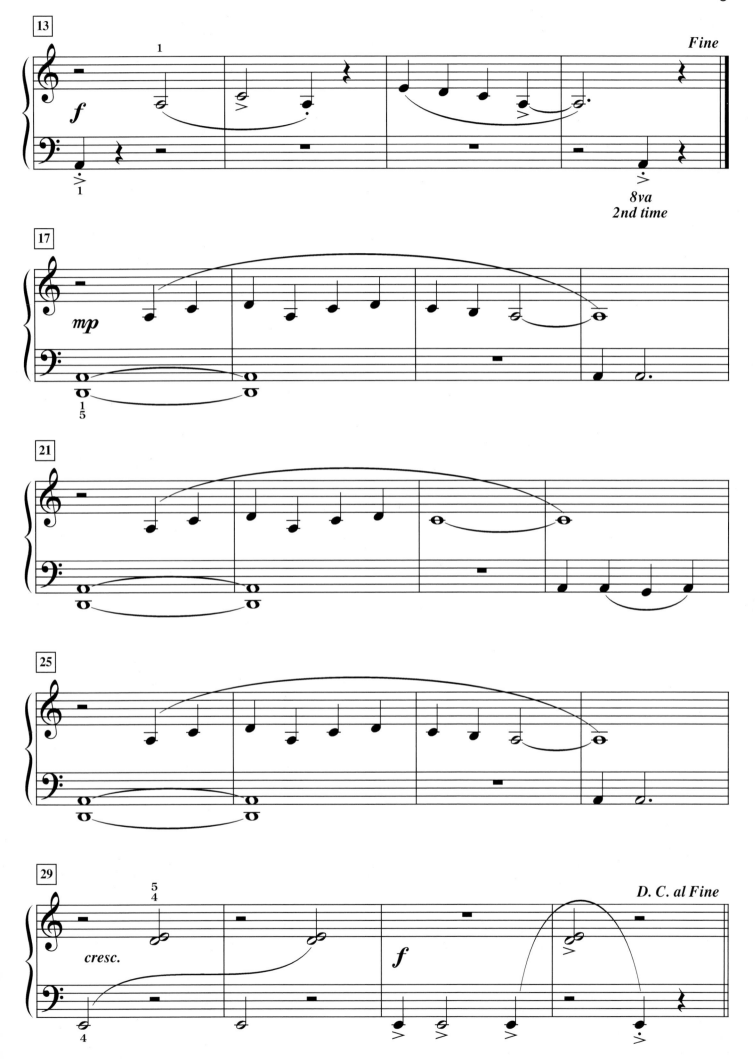

Both hands play only black keys throughout.

1. Compare mm. 1–4 with mm. 5–8.
   Only one note is different. Name the note. _____

   In which measures is this note found? _____

2. Compare mm. 9–12 with mm. 13–16.
   Only one note is different. Name the note. _____

   In which measures is this note found? _____

On Butterfly Wings

At a leisurely pace ($\quad$ = ca. 76)
Both hands 8va throughout
Both hands 15ma 2nd time

Robert D. Vandall

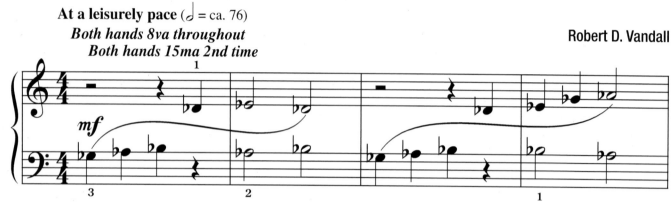

Press damper pedal and hold throughout (without duet)

Optional Duet Part:

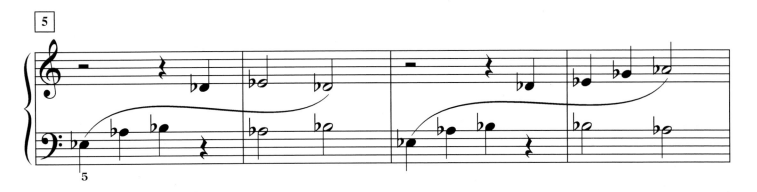

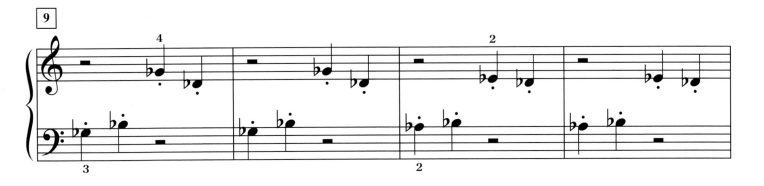

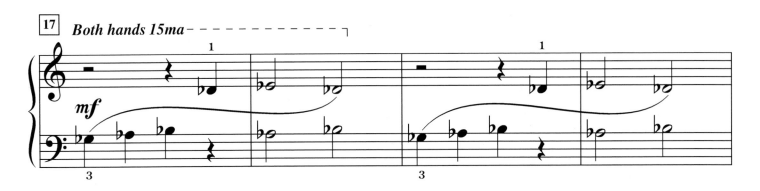

This piece is in G mixolydian.

1. There are two different harmonic intervals in this piece. Name the intervals. _____

   In which measures are these intervals found? _____

2. Both hands use five different five-finger patterns. Name these patterns. _____

Contrasts

Fast and bouncy (♩ = ca. 116)

Robert D. Vandall

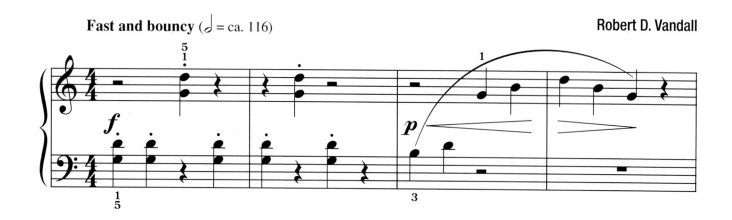

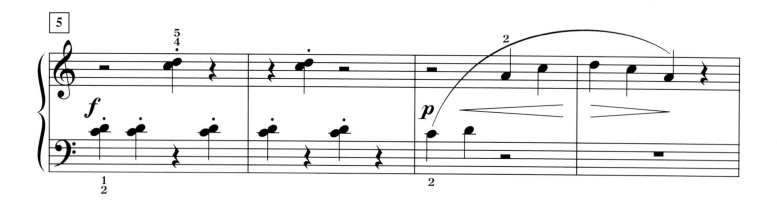

TAKE NOTE

This piece is in C major.

1. There are two different harmonic
    intervals in this piece. Name the intervals. _____

    In which measures are these intervals found? _____

2. The E♭ changes the key from C major
    to C minor. Which measures have E♭? _____

3. The way the melody is phrased can change how
    the rhythm feels. Which measures have two-note slurs? _____
    How do these slurs change the feel of the rhythm?

    _____

Chocolate Swirls

Quickly, with a graceful lilt (♩ = ca. 184)

Robert D. Vandall

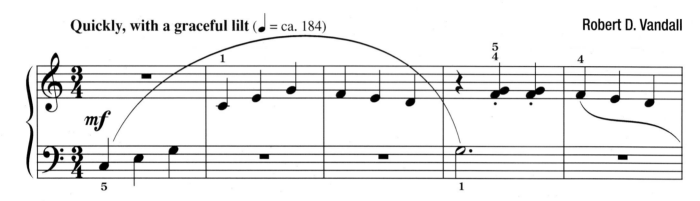

Optional Duet Part: Student plays one octave higher.

Quickly, with a graceful lilt (♩ = ca. 184)

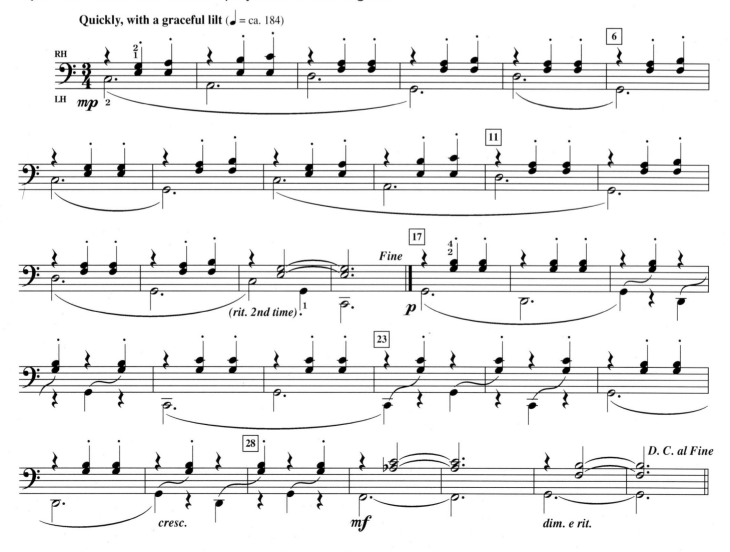

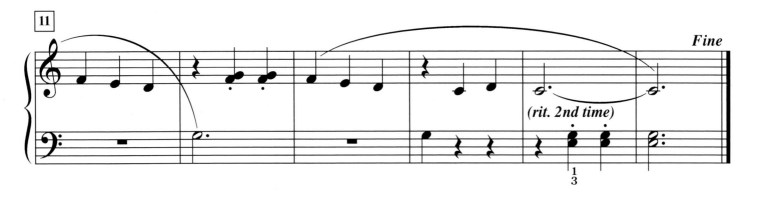

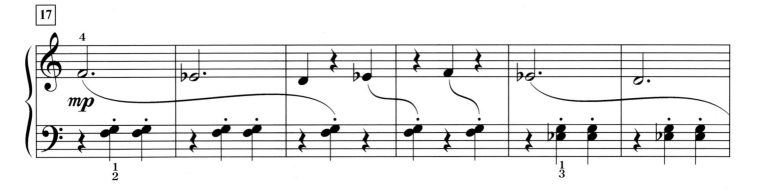

This piece is in C major.

1.   The right hand and left hand mirror
     each other in mm. 1–8. In which other
     measures do they mirror each other? _____

2.   All notes are played staccato, except for
     the notes that are marked "tenuto."
     Which measures have tenuto markings? _____

3.   Both hands use three different five-finger
     patterns. Name these patterns. _____

Robot on the Keys

Unyieldingly steady and fast (♩ = ca. 176)

Robert D. Vandall

Optional Duet Part: Student plays two octaves higher.

Unyieldingly steady and fast (♩ = ca. 176)

This piece is in E minor.

1. The left hand stays in an E five-finger pattern for the entire piece, but the right hand changes patterns. What five-finger patterns does the right hand use? _____

2. Compare the right hand in mm. 1–8 with mm. 9–16. Is it the same or different? _____

Morning Fog

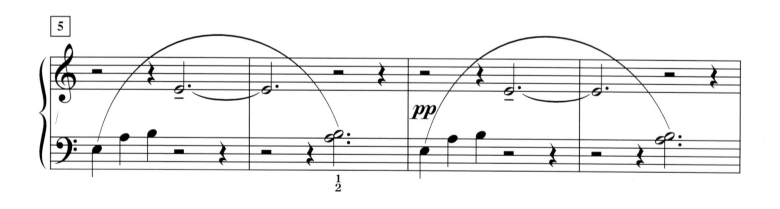

14

This piece is in D minor.

1. Both thumbs begin on D.
   Do the thumbs play any note other than D? _____

2. The right-hand pattern in mm. 1–2
   is repeated throughout the piece.
   How many times is this pattern used? _____

3. Compare the left hand in mm. 1–8 with
   mm. 9–16. Which measures are different? _____

Jazzman

Robert D. Vandall

Not too fast (♩ = ca. 104)

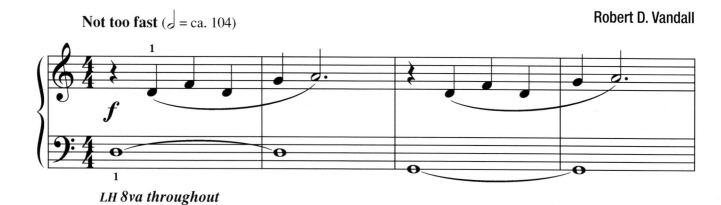

LH 8va throughout

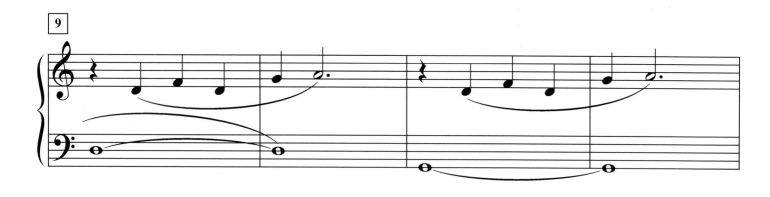

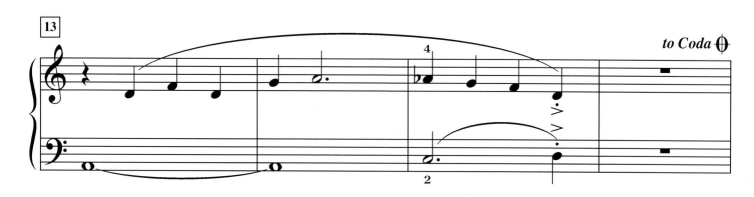

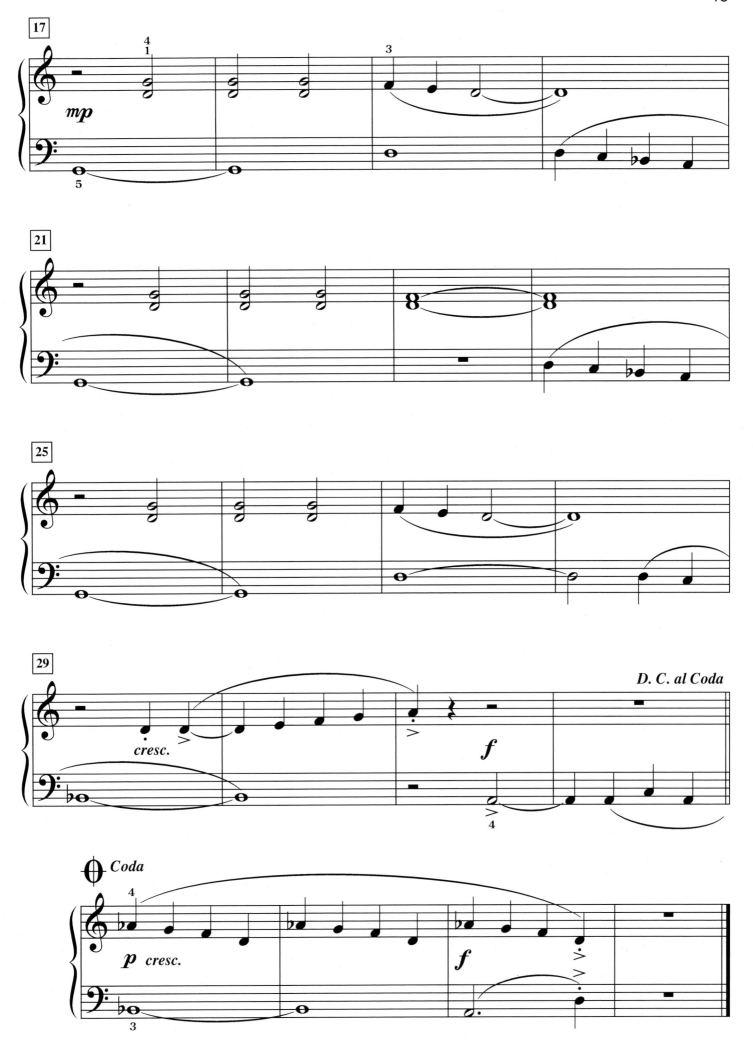

This piece shifts between D major and D minor.

1. The right-hand third finger alternates
    between two different notes. Name these notes. _____

2. Compare the left hand in mm. 5–8
    with mm. 13–16. How are they different?

    _____

Scary Story

Frightfully fast (♩ = ca. 176)

Robert D. Vandall

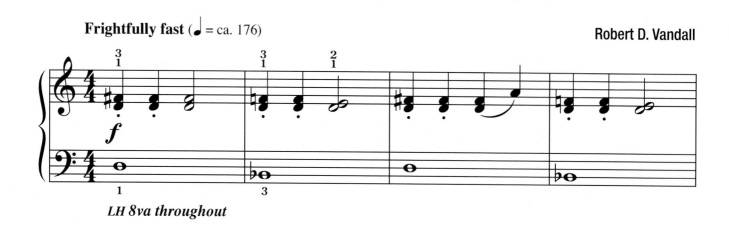

LH 8va throughout

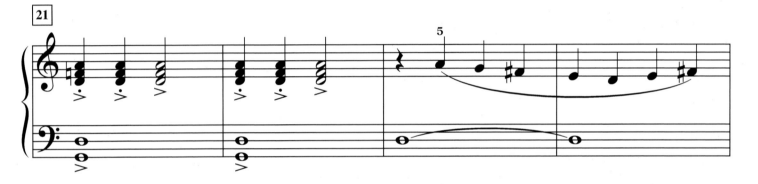

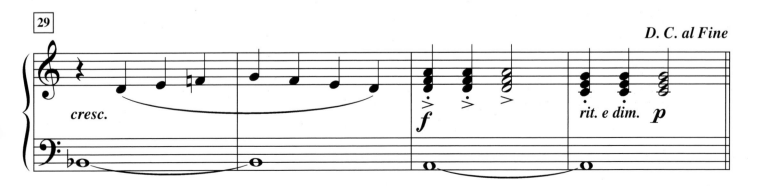

TAKE NOTE

This piece is in C major.

1. The right-hand thumb remains on middle C for the entire piece except in one measure. Name the measure where the right-hand thumb is not on C. _____

2. The left hand uses two different five-finger patterns. Name these patterns. _____

3. The right-hand third finger alternates between two different notes. Name these notes. _____

Blue Boogie

Fast, strong and steady (♩ = ca. 176)

Robert D. Vandall

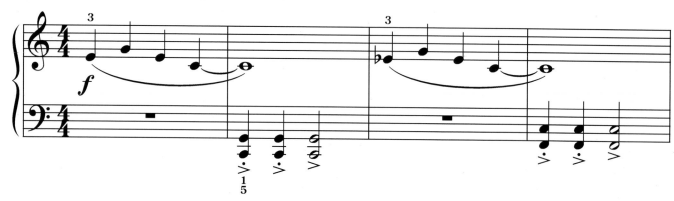

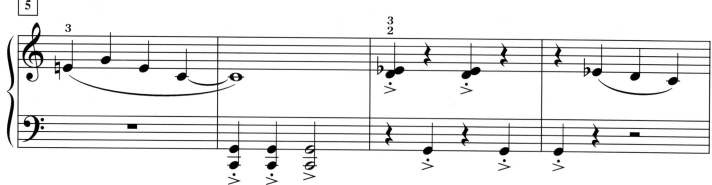

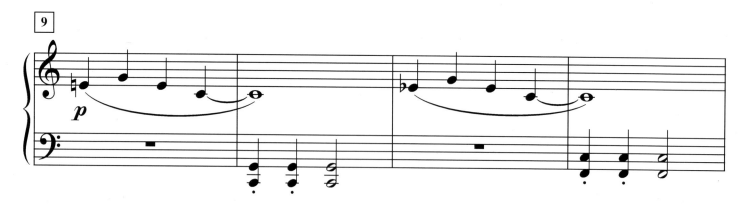

TAKE NOTE

This piece is in G major.

1. Compare mm. 1-8 with mm. 9-16. How are they the same?

   _____

   How are they different? _____

2. In which measures does the right hand play harmonic 2nds? _____

3. Both hands use three different five-finger patterns.

   Name these patterns._____

Barn Dance

Robert D. Vandall

Fast and strongly rhythmic (♩ = ca. 120)

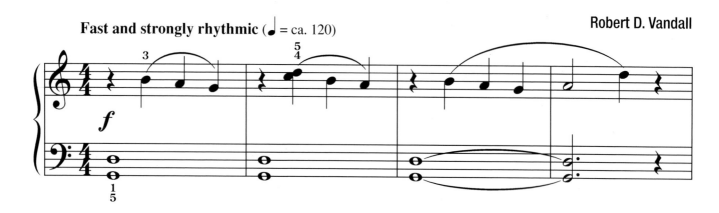

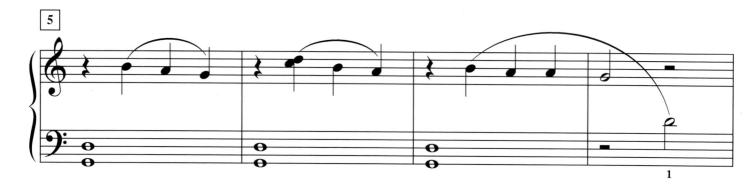

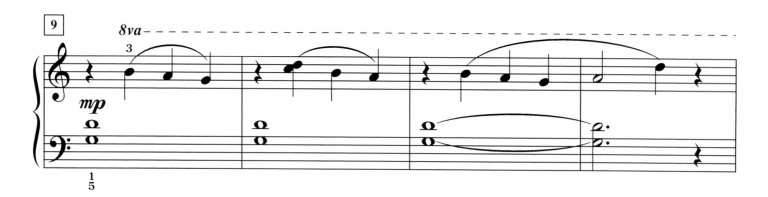

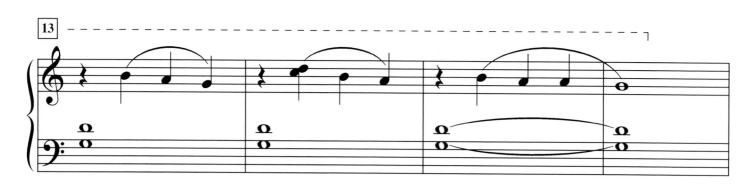

This piece is in F major.

1. This piece uses four different
   harmonic intervals. Name these intervals. _____

2. The right-hand pattern in mm. 3-4 is repeated
   throughout the piece. How many times is this pattern used? _____

3. Compare the left hand mm. 17-24 with
   mm. 25-32. What is different about mm. 25-32?

Freeway Frenzy

Robert D. Vandall

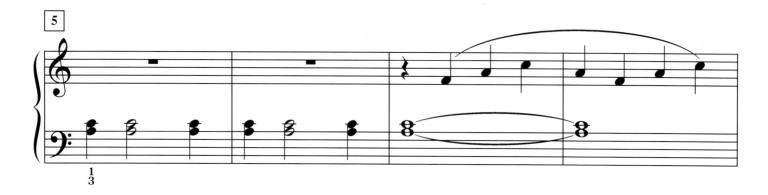

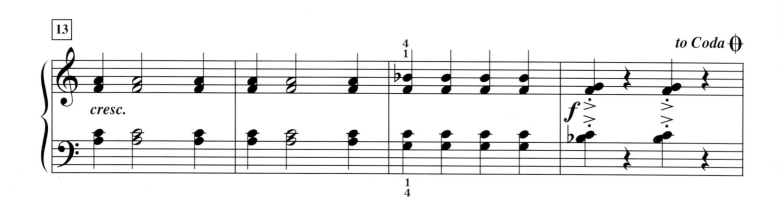

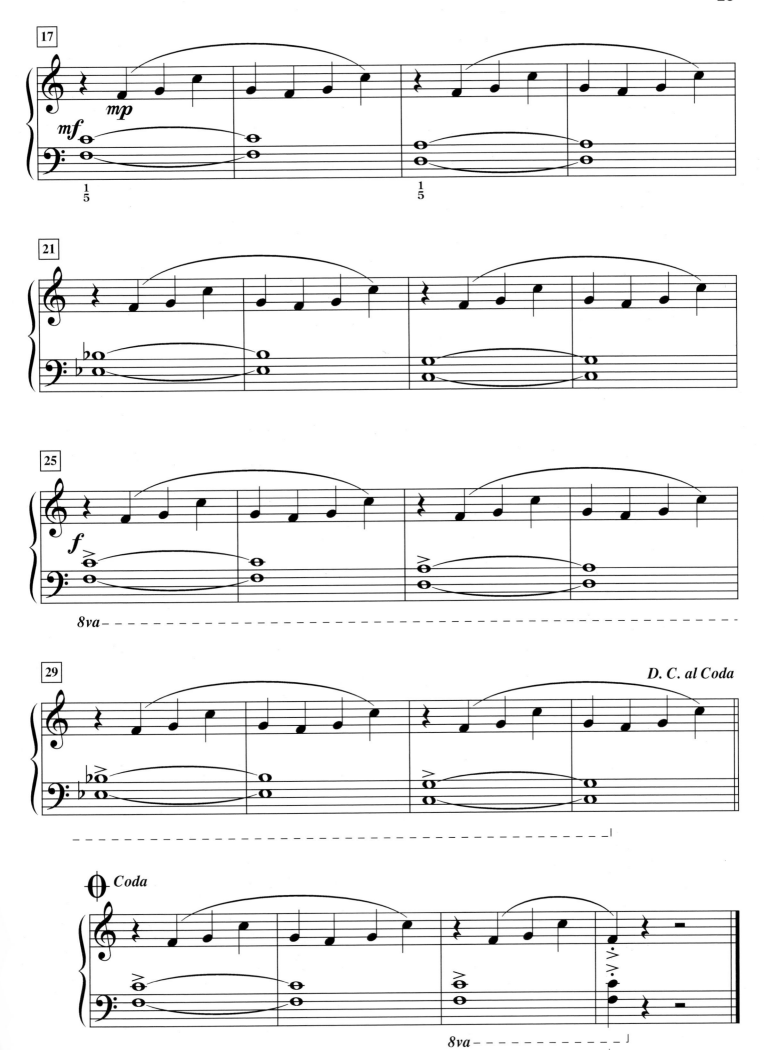